THE DART OF
LONGING LOVE

Daily Readings from
The Cloud of Unknowing
and *The Epistle of Privy Counsel*

Introduced and rendered into modern English by:
ROBERT LLEWELYN

DARTON · LONGMAN + TODD

First published in 1983 by
Darton, Longman and Todd Ltd
1 Spencer Court
140–142 Wandsworth High Street
London SW18 4JJ

First edition reprinted 1985, 1987, 1990 and 1994
This second edition 2004

ISBN 0–232–52553–6

A catalogue record for this book is available from
the British Library

Designed by Sandie Boccacci
Typeset by Intype Libra Ltd
Printed and bound in Great Britain by
William Clowes, Beccles, Suffolk

Contents

The Cloud *and its author*

The Dart of Longing Love is offered as a companion volume to the warmly received book of devotional readings: *Enfolded in Love*. It seeks to do for *The Cloud of Unknowing* what the other book does for Mother Julian's *Revelations of Divine Love*. In its pages will be found the heart of *The Cloud* and, it is hoped, all that is needed to enable those with a drawing to the way of contemplative prayer to pursue their calling, supported by the encouragement and wisdom which *The Cloud* provides. The present book is probably best read straight through in two or three sessions, and then – for those who wish to savour it more slowly – it may be taken daily over the period of one or two months for which it is designed.

Several passages, mainly contemporary, have been added after the completed daily readings. They can be read at any stage and may perhaps be helpful to those who have not hitherto been acquainted with the way of *The Cloud*. The language of spirituality changes from one generation to another while the underlying experience remains the same. It is thus with *The Cloud*. If in places its style seems outmoded – even when clothed in modern dress – the experience to which it points is unvaried, and it may be judged that few have known that experience in such depth and intensity as the unknown author of this fourteenth-century work. The additional passages referred to tell of the same journey, and those who can relate to them may be reassured that they are on the road of which *The Cloud* speaks. The sources from which they are taken are shown at the end of the book, and here I may simply make grateful acknowledgement to authors and publishers for allowing them to be reproduced.

It is not possible to supply any precise date for *The Cloud*. It has always been placed in the second half of the fourteenth century, and recent research seems to indicate that it was not later than the seventh decade. Its authorship is equally obscure. There is no evidence for the author's name and no certainty of his way of life. It has been conjectured that he was a Cistercian hermit or a Carthusian priest. Some support to the view that he was a priest is supplied in that the author leaves the reader with his blessing at the end of *The Cloud*. This, too, applies to two other of his works. We may certainly judge from the writings themselves that he was a well-versed theologian and an experienced director of souls.

The language, we are told, is that of the East Midlands of the period, indicating an abode in the Lincolnshire area. The style reveals a man of vigorous and lively mind, vivid in imagination and a keen observer of his fellow-men. One can hardly be wrong in presenting the author as a man of exceptionally attractive and gracious personality, according well, one would imagine, with the description on page 55 of those practised in his 'work'.

The Cloud is addressed to a young man of twenty-four who had received the contemplative call after a period in the 'active' Christian life. Through him, we may infer from the prologue, it is addressed to all who are similarly called. This is also true of *The Epistle of Privy Counsel* which is written in the first place for the same person, and from which a few readings have been taken in the pages which follow. *Privy Counsel* may be seen as an appendix to *The Cloud*, more mature, as we would expect, both author and disciple having naturally developed in the spiritual life.

In rendering the text into modern English I have had to work to the discipline of the single page and, so far as possible, to make each reading speak for itself. This has involved the occasional taking of minor liberties which would not be justifiable in a full translation of the work. A sentence of recapitulation not in the original has sometimes been necessary, and even within paragraphs omissions have been made. I have felt that to insert dots to indicate this would impede the free flow and perhaps be tedious to the reader. The book is clearly not intended to take the place of a complete edition of *The Cloud* – even where the passages overlap – and such liberties will not seem inappropriate. The reader should, however, be informed.

The author of *The Cloud* is at pains to emphasize that not every Christian – at least not here and now – has the call to this work. The summons may indeed come later. Once it has come, the *things* of God – what the author calls his attributes or qualities – must be left behind in the quest for God *himself*. A time for reflective meditation there must always be, but we shall know that our real prayer life lies beyond. 'By love he may be gotten and holden, by thought never.' These often-quoted words from *The Cloud* take us to the heart of its teaching.

ROBERT LLEWELYN
The Julian Shrine
c/o All Hallows
Rouen Road
Norwich

Smite upon that thick cloud of unknowing
with a sharp dart of longing love.
Come what may, do not give up.
(The Cloud of Unknowing, ch. 6)

Called to Contemplation

Look up, you feckless creature, and take a good look at yourself! What are you, and what have you done to deserve to be called in this way by our Lord? How tired and wretched the heart, and sunken deep in laziness, which will not be awakened by the drawing of this love and the voice of this calling!

Be warned, you miserable man, lest you consider yourself to be more holy or virtuous on account of your high calling and the singular nature of your life.

You are but the more pitiable if you fail to avail yourself of counsel and grace to live in godliness according to your vocation.

Your spiritual spouse, that is Almighty God, King of Kings and Lord of Lords, humbles himself for you. Can you do less for him?

Out of all his followers, he most graciously chooses you to be one of his special disciples.

A Whole-hearted Commitment

Press on quickly, I beg you. Look to the future and leave the past behind.

See what you lack and not what you have, for that is the quickest path to humility.

You must always be wanting God if you are to move forward to perfection.

This desire must at all times be at work in your will by the power of Almighty God, and with your own consent.

But mark this well: he is a jealous lover and brooks no rivals. He has no wish to work within you unless he can be there alone.

He asks no help, but only you yourself.

God Is Waiting for You

He wants you simply to look on him and to allow him to act alone.

Let your part be to guard the windows and the door against the onslaught of flies and enemies.

If you are prepared to do this you have only to prevail upon him with prayer, and he will soon come to your help.

Work on, then, and let us see how you manage. He himself is always most willing and simply awaits you.

What are you going to do, and how are you going to lay hold on him?

The Work which Pleases God Most

Lift up your heart to God with a humble stirring of love; and mean God himself, and not what you get from him.

Be on your guard lest you think of anything but God himself. Let nothing occupy your mind or will but only God.

Do everything you can to forget all God's creatures and their activities, so that nothing holds your mind or desire whether it be in general or particular.

Let them be, and pay no attention to them.

This is the work of the soul which pleases God more than any other. All saints and angels rejoice over it, and speed it on with all their might.

All mankind is wonderfully helped by this work – more than you can ever be aware. Yes, even the very souls in purgatory find their pains eased by virtue of it.

And you yourself are made clean and virtuous by this work as by no other.

A Cloud of Unknowing

In the power of grace, and in the strength of eager and joyful desire, this is the lightest work of all. Otherwise it is hard, and a wonder if you achieve it.

Work away, then, until desire is kindled. When you first begin you will find only darkness and, as it were, a cloud of unknowing.

You cannot tell what it is, excepting that you feel in your will a naked reaching out to God.

This cloud and this darkness, no matter what you do, is between you and your God. It prevents you from seeing him clearly with your mind and from experiencing the sweetness of his love in your heart.

Prepare yourself to wait in this darkness as long as you may, ever calling after him whom you love.

If ever you shall feel him or see him – as far as is possible here below – it must always be in this cloud and this darkness.

If you will but work on earnestly as I bid you, I believe that in his mercy you will win through.

A Power to Know and a Power to Love

All rational creatures, whether angels or men, have within them the capacity to know and the capacity to love.

In the exercise of the power of knowledge God must ever remain incomprehensible.

Whereas in the exercise of love he may be fully comprehended.

So much so that a loving soul, by virtue of love, may comprehend him who is all sufficient to fill all the souls of men and angels that could ever be.

This is the marvellous unending miracle of love.

Man Was Made for this Work

If any man were so transformed by grace as to respond at all times to the stirrings of his will, he would never be – even in this life – without some taste of the divine sweetness; and he would experience its consummation in the joys of heaven.

It is in man's very nature to be subject to these stirrings; so do not be surprised that I should urge you to this work.

This is the work, as you shall later hear, which man would have faithfully pursued if he had never sinned.

Man was made for this work, and by it he shall be made whole. So, too, for want of it he will fall ever more deeply into sin; and he will increasingly distance himself from God.

By faithfully pursuing this work – and none other – a man is progressively set free from the dominion of sin and grows ever closer to God.

For the Love of Jesus

Be watchful of time and how you spend it. Nothing is more precious than time. In the twinkling of an eye heaven may be won or lost.

Time is made for man, not man for time.

I hear you say sadly, 'How shall I fare? And if what you say is true, how shall I give account of each moment of time? – I, who am now twenty-four, and until now have never paid heed to time . . . Help me now for the love of Jesus.'

That is indeed well said: 'For the love of Jesus.' For in the love of Jesus you shall find your help.

So then love Jesus, and all that he has is yours. Knit yourself to him by love and faith.

As a Spark from the Fire

Pay careful heed to this work and to its wonderful manner of operation within your soul.

If it be rightly understood it is none other than a sudden stirring – coming without warning – leaping up to God as a spark from the fire.

Marvellous also are the number of stirrings which in a single hour may be effected in a soul disposed to this work.

Yet in but a single one, a man may have suddenly and completely forgotten every created thing.

Equally quickly, after each stirring, on account of the corruption of our nature, the soul may fall back to some thought or deed, real or imagined.

But what of it? For it quickly leaps up again as suddenly as before.

The Nature of the Darkness

You are not to think that when I refer to this darkness as a cloud, it is to be regarded as a cloud formed from the vapours floating in the air, nor yet as any darkness such as you know in your house at night when the candle is out.

Such a darkness or cloud you could conjure up in your imagination, seeing it before your eyes on the brightest summer day.

Equally, on the darkest winter night you could imagine a brightly shining light.

Drop such fancies. I mean nothing of the kind.

When I use the word 'darkness' I mean a lack of knowing: just as everything which you do not know, or which you have forgotten, is dark to you; for you do not see it in your mind's eye.

For this reason this darkness which is between you and your God, I do not call a cloud of the air, but a cloud of unknowing.

The Cloud of Forgetting

Just as this cloud of unknowing is above you and between you and your God, so too you must put a cloud of forgetting beneath you and between you and all created things.

It may, perhaps, seem to you that you are a long way off from God because of this cloud of unknowing between you and him.

But surely, if the truth be told, you are much further from him when you have no cloud of forgetting between him and all his creatures.

When I speak of God's creatures I mean not them only, whether bodily or spiritual, but also their state and their works, whether good or evil.

In short, I tell you, everything is to be hidden under the cloud of forgetting.

Nothing but God Alone

Although it is very profitable sometimes to think of the state and works of some of God's creatures, yet in this work it profits little or nothing at all.

Why is this so? It is because to remember or think of any creature – or of its deeds – is a sort of spiritual light. The eye of your soul is opened to it – and even fastened on it – as the marksman's eye is upon the centre of the target at which he shoots.

Let me impress this one thing upon you: that every single thing on which you may think is for the time being above you and between you and your God.

You will distance yourself from God to the extent that there is anything in your mind excepting God alone.

The Naked Being of God

If it may be said courteously and fittingly, it profits little or nothing in this work to think of the kindness or worthiness of God, nor of our Lady, nor of the saints or angels in heaven, nor yet of the joys of heaven: that is to say with a special looking towards them as if you would thereby find nourishment to help you in your task.

I believe that it would not in any way assist this work. For although it is good to think upon the kindness of God, and to love him and praise him for it, it is far better to think upon his naked being, and to love him and praise him for himself.

A Sharp Dart of Longing Love

Of God himself no man can think. He may well be loved, but not thought.

By love he may be grasped and held; by thought never.

Although it is good at times to think specially of the kindness and goodness of God, and although this may enlighten you and play a part in contemplation, nevertheless in this work such thoughts shall be put down and covered with a cloud of forgetting.

You are to step above them boldly and eagerly, and with a devout and lively impulse of love you are to try to pierce the darkness above you.

Smite upon that thick cloud of unknowing with a sharp dart of longing love.

Come what may, do not give up.

Him I Covet, Him I Seek, and Him Alone

❧

If any thought should arise and continually press above you and between you and the darkness, and if it should say to you: 'What are you looking for? What would you have?', then make answer that it is God whom you would have.

'Him I covet, him I seek, and him alone.'

And if the thought should ask you, 'What is that God?', then you are to say that it is the God who made you, and bought you, and who has graciously called you to his love.

'And in him', you may say to this thought, 'you have no power over me.'

Therefore say to him, 'Get down again,' and tread him down quickly with a stirring of love.

You are to do this even though he seems to you to be a truly holy thought, and even though it seems that he would help you to seek God.

A Scattered Mind

It may well be that the thought will bring to your mind a variety of striking and lovely instances of God's kindness. Perhaps he will say that God is all sweetness, all loving, all gracious and all merciful.

He wants nothing better than that you should listen to him. He will then tease you more and more, bringing you down lower and lower.

Eventually he will bring to your mind our Lord's Passion, wherein he will let you see the wonderful kindness of God. And if you listen to him he wants nothing better.

For it will not be long before he lets you see your old wretched life, bringing to mind perhaps some place in which you once lived.

And at the end, before you know what is happening to you, your mind will be scattered, you know not where.

And all this dissipation simply because you listened to him willingly at first, and then answered him and received him, and allowed him to have his way.

The Time for Meditation Is Past

Nevertheless, what the thought said was both good and holy.

Yes, indeed, and so holy that if any man or woman should think to come to contemplation without experiencing earlier in their life many devout meditations on their own wretchedness, the Passion, the kindness, the great goodness and worthiness of God, they will surely err and fail in this exercise.

Nevertheless it is necessary for a man or woman who has been accustomed to such meditations over a long period to leave them behind, and to put them down and hold them down under a cloud of forgetting, if they are ever to pierce the cloud of unknowing between them and their God.

And so, whenever you exercise yourself in this work, feeling that you are called of God's grace, raise your heart to God with a humble stirring of love. Mean God who made you and bought you, and has graciously called you to this work, and allow no other thought of God.

Yet even this is not necessary. For it suffices that you should reach out with a naked intent to God with no desire but himself.

A Short Word to Be Kept Intact

If it suits you, you can have this naked intent wrapped up and enfolded in one word. In that case, in order that you may have a better grasp on it, take a short word of one syllable. One syllable is better than two, and the shorter the word the more suited it is to accomplish the work of the spirit.

Such a word is the word 'God' or the word 'Love'. Choose whichever you wish, or another if you prefer, but let it be of one syllable.

Fasten this word to your heart so that it never leaves you, come what may. This word is to be your shield and your spear, whether in peace or in war.

With this word you are to beat upon the cloud and the darkness above you. With it you are to smite down every manner of thought under the cloud of forgetting. So much so, that if any thought should press upon you to ask you what you would have, answer it with no other words but this one word.

And if you should be tempted to analyse this word, answer that you will have it whole and un-developed. If you will but hold fast, be sure that the temptation will not last long.

God to Be Loved for Himself

It is more profitable for the health of your soul, more worthy in itself, and more pleasing to God and the saints and angels in heaven, and more helpful too to all your friends, bodily or spiritual, living or dead, to experience a blind stirring of love towards God for his own sake, and a secret pressing upon this cloud of unknowing – known and felt in spiritual desire – than to have your inward eye opened in contemplating or beholding all the angels or saints in heaven, or in hearing all the merriment and melody which accompanies their bliss.

But be assured that no man shall have that clear sight in this life; though through the grace of God you may experience feelings in your affection, that is when God chooses to give them. So lift up your love to that cloud, or as I would prefer to say, let God draw your love to it, and endeavour through God's grace to forget everything else.

An Involuntary Thought not Sinful

A spontaneous thought of any living man or woman, or of some thing, making an impression on your will or understanding, cannot be counted as sin. This is beyond your control, and is the painful effect of original sin of which you were cleansed in your baptism.

Nevertheless, if this sudden stirring or thought is not quickly beaten down, your carnal heart, by reason of its frailty, will be immediately disturbed by some kind of affection if the thing is something which pleases you or has pleased you in the past; or else by some sort of resentment, if it be something on which you imagine you have a grievance or have had one before.

An affection of this sort may be grave in the case of worldly living men and women who have hitherto lived in serious sin. But in you and in all others who have sincerely desired to renounce the world, and are bound to a life of godliness within the Church, whether privately or openly, under guidance and authority – such an affection or grievance is but venial sin.

The reason for this is the rooting and grounding of your intention in God, made when you began your life in the state in which you now stand firm.

Wrath, Envy and Sloth

If the affection or resentment which attaches itself to your fleshly heart be allowed to remain for a while unreproached, so that it eventually attaches itself to your spiritual heart – by which I mean your will – with your full consent: then it is mortal sin.

This takes place when you, or any of those of whom I am speaking, voluntarily draw to themselves the memory of any living man or woman, or of any material or worldly thing.

If this memory is of something which grieves you or has grieved you in the past, there will rise within you feelings of anger and a desire for revenge. This is known as *wrath*.

Or there may arise a vehement contempt and a degree of loathing for some person, and with it spiteful and judgemental thoughts. This is *envy*.

Or yet again it may be a weariness and boredom for any good employment, whether bodily or spiritual. This is *sloth*.

Pride, Covetousness, Gluttony and Lust

If what presents itself is something which pleases you or has pleased you in the past, there will be a fleeting enticement to think on it, whatever it may be. So much so, that you may rest in it and finally fix your heart and will to it, and feed your carnal heart upon it, thinking for the time being that you desire no other pleasure but ever to live with it in peace and rest.

If this thought which you are encouraging, or it may be that it has presented itself and you have simply accepted it and now rest in it with relish, is one concerned with physical or intellectual gifts, or honour or rank, or charm or beauty, then it is *pride*.

If it be a thought of any kind of worldly possessions, riches or property, or whatever a man may have or control, then it is *covetousness*.

If it concerns delicacies of food or wine, or any of the delights of the palate, it is *gluttony*.

If it be love, or pleasure, or any manner of flirtation, or the fondling or flattering of any man or woman, or of yourself either, then it is *lust*.

Carelessness in Small Sins

I do not say this because I believe that you or any other of whom I speak are guilty or burdened with any such sins, but because I want you to estimate each thought and impulse at its true worth; and also to work hard to put down the first stirring of each thought which may lead you into sin.

Let me tell you this: he who does not weigh, or sets little store by the first thought – even if to him it be no sin – shall not escape carelessness in venial sin.

No man can be completely free from venial sin in this mortal life. But carelessness in venial sin should always be avoided by all true disciples of perfection; otherwise it is little wonder that they soon fall into mortal sin.

Sin Destroyed at Its Roots

If, then, you would stand and not fall, never set your intention aside, but strike always with a sharp dart of longing love upon this cloud of unknowing which is between you and your God; and hate to think of anything less than God, and do not leave your work for any reason whatever.

Of all works, it alone – and of itself – destroys sin at its roots.

No matter how much you fast, how long you watch, how early you rise, how hard your bed, how rough your clothes – all this will not help you a whit. The impulse and stirring of sin will still be in you.

And yet more. No matter how much you weep in sorrow for your sins, or for the Passion of Christ, and no matter how much you are mindful of the joys of heaven, although you would find here much good, help, profit and grace, yet in comparison with this blind stirring of love – or without it – it can do but little.

Purification of Motive

This blind impulse of love not only destroys the root and ground of sin so far as is possible in this life, but it also begets the virtues.

All virtue is thereby delicately infused, and is known and experienced without any corruption of motive.

No matter how many virtues a man may have, they will be imperfect and in some degree tainted unless they are rooted in this work.

Virtue is nothing else but an ordered and measured affection directed towards God for his sake alone.

He himself is the foundation of all virtues; so much so that if any man be stirred to any one virtue by a mixture of motives – even though God himself be the chief – then that virtue is imperfect.

The two virtues, humility and charity, are good examples and may stand for the others. Whoever has these clearly needs no more. For he has them all.

True Humility Flows from God Alone

Let us look first at the virtue of humility.

It is imperfect when it originates from anything other than God, even though God be the chief source. It is perfect when it flows from God himself.

In itself humility is a true knowledge and awareness of oneself as one really is. It is undoubtedly true that if any man could see and know himself as he is, he would be truly humble.

There are two sources from which humility springs. The first is the depravity and wretchedness and weakness of man, into which state he has fallen through sin. In some degree he must always be aware of this throughout his life, however holy he may be.

The second source is the overwhelming love and goodness of God himself, at the sight of which nature trembles, learned men are fools and saints and angels blinded.

The second is perfect; and that is because it will last for ever.

The Nature of Charity

Charity means nothing else but to love God for himself above all creatures, and to love one's fellow-men for God's sake even as one loves oneself.

It is entirely right and fitting that in this work God should be loved for himself and above all creation. For, as has been noted earlier, the essential nature of this work is nothing other than a naked intent directed to God for his sake only.

I call it a naked intent because in this work the perfect apprentice does not ask for remission of pain, nor for a greater reward, nor in short for anything but God himself.

It is even true that he neither takes notice nor considers whether he is in pain or in joy, but is concerned simply that the will of God whom he loves is fulfilled.

Thus, in this work God is perfectly loved for himself, and above all creation. In it the perfect worker may not allow the memory of the holiest creature God ever made to have any share in what is being done.

No Man a Stranger

❦

It is clearly true that in this work the second and lower part of charity, that of loving one's fellow-Christian, is truly and perfectly fulfilled.

The reason is that the perfect worker has no special regard for any particular person whether relative or stranger, friend or foe.

He thinks of all men alike as his kinsmen and none as strangers. He sees all as friends and none as enemies.

So much is this so, that he regards all who hurt and maltreat him in this life as his best and special friends; and he believes that he is moved to will them as much good as to his most intimate friend.

All will be loved genuinely and sincerely for God; as too will he love himself.

He who would be a perfect disciple of our Lord must ardently lift up his spirit in this spiritual work on behalf of all mankind, as did our Lord in his body on the cross.

A Beam of Spiritual Light

Work hard then, and beat upon this high cloud of unknowing; afterwards you may rest. Anyone who takes on this work unless he be given special grace, or has been long accustomed to it, will find it hard indeed.

The demanding nature of this work is to be found in the putting down of the memory of creatures and in holding them under the cloud of forgetting. This is man's work with the help of grace. The stirring of love, that is God's work. So press on and do your part, and I promise that he will not fail in his.

Work away then. Work hard for a while and the burden will soon be lightened. For although it is hard in the beginning when you lack devotion, after a while when devotion is kindled it will become restful and light.

God will sometimes work all by himself, though not for long at a time and only when and how he wills. You will then be happily content to let him work alone.

It may be that sometimes he will send out a beam of spiritual light piercing the cloud of unknowing that is between you and him, showing you some of his secrets, of which man may not and cannot speak.

Who Should Engage in this Work

If you ask me who should take part in this work, I answer: all who have truly forsaken the world, and who are giving themselves to the contemplative rather than the active life; all such, whoever they may be, and whether in the past they have been habitual sinners or not, should persevere in this work.

But if you ask me when they should begin, then I answer: not until they have cleansed their consciences, through the accustomed rites of the Church, of all the occasions of past sin.

The root and ground of sin which remains in the soul after confession, however thorough this may be, is dried up in this work.

So then when you feel you have done all you can to amend yourself at the bar of Holy Church, set yourself quickly to this work. And if it be that memories of your past actions continually press between you and your God – or any new thought or impulse of sin – you shall steadfastly step over them with an ardent stirring of love, and tread them down under your feet.

Try to cover them with a thick cloud of forgetting. As often as they rise, put them down.

Look over Their Shoulder

There are various secret devices and techniques which you may use to put away intruding thoughts and memories if you find the going is very hard. These are better learnt from God and tested in your own experience than from any living person.

Nevertheless I shall tell you as much of this as I think wise. Try it out, and improve on it if you can.

Do everything that is in you to behave as if you did not know that the memories and thoughts press between you and God.

Try to look over their shoulders seeking something else, which is God shrouded in the cloud of unknowing. If you do this, I believe that in a short while your work will be eased.

I believe that if this device is well and truly understood, it is nothing else but a longing desire for God, to feel him and see him as far as may be in this life.

Such a desire is charity, and it always makes for a lightening of your work.

Abandonment into God's Hands

Let me give you another dodge. Test it if you will.

When you find that you can in no way put your thoughts down, cower beneath them as a faint-hearted prisoner overcome in war, and consider that it is but folly to do battle with them any longer.

In this way you surrender yourself to God in the hands of your enemies. Even as you do it, imagine yourself to be conquered for ever.

I beg you to take good note of this advice for I believe that in the testing of it your problem will vanish as though dissolving in water. And I truly believe that if this stratagem be rightly understood, it is nothing other than a true knowledge and awareness of yourself as you are, a foul wretch far worse than nothing.

This knowledge and awareness is humility. Its effect will be to bring God down to you in power to avenge you of your enemies, and to lift you up and lovingly dry your spiritual tears, just as a father rescues his child who is at the point of perishing at the mouths of wild boars or mad, biting bears.

It Is Your Purgatory

I will not speak of more devices just now; for if you have the grace to test these, I believe that you will be able to teach me better than I can teach you.

For although it is as I have said, yet I truly believe that I am very far from the goal myself; and therefore I pray that you will help me, and that you will work for me, as too for yourself.

I urge you then to press on and work hard. Suffer humbly the pain you meet by the way, for truly it is your purgatory.

At last when suffering is behind you, and your skills are given by God and by his grace have become habitual, I have no doubt that you will be cleansed not only from sin but also from the pain of sin – I mean the pain of specific sins, and not the pain of original sin which must remain with you until you die, however hard you may work.

You will continually experience fresh impulses as the effect of original sin, and as often as they arise you are to strike them down.

Let God Work as He Will

Let this way of prayer form you and lead you where it will. Let it do the shaping; your part is to submit. Watch it if you like, but let it be. Do not interfere in an attempt to help; you are more likely to spoil everything.

Let it be the carpenter and you the wood; it the householder and you the house.

Be content to dwell in darkness and to renounce all desire of knowledge, for that will hinder more than help.

It is enough that you are moved lovingly – by what you do not know – and that you have no thought of anything less than God and that your desire is nakedly directed to God alone.

If it be as I have described, you may confidently believe that it is God only who is acting upon your will; and directly so, without any exterior supports.

Meditation Leading to Prayer

There are three stages which the beginner should note. I call these reading, reflecting and praying. Others have written of them better than I can, and I need not say much of them here.

But this I will tell you. Note, however, that I am writing now for beginners and proficients; it is otherwise for the 'perfect', so far as that word can be used of men in this life. These three employments are linked, reading coming first and leading to reflection, and reflection in its turn giving place to prayer.

There is, too, hearing; but this I take to be the same as reading. Thus clergy read books and the laity 'read' the clergy when they hear them preach. In reality it is all one.

Without the reading or hearing of God's word it is impossible for a man blinded by sin to see the foul spot on his conscience.

It is then and not before that he runs to the well to wash. If the spot be due to some deliberate sin, then the well is the Church and the water confession. If it be but a blind root and stirring of sin, then the well is God most merciful, and the water is prayer with all that it entails.

The Contemplative Way

🙚

It is, however, otherwise for those who give themselves continually to the work of this book. For them, in place of formal meditation, there is simply a spontaneous awareness of their wretchedness or of God's goodness; and this without any previous reading or hearing, or reflection upon anything at all. What I now speak of is better learnt of God than of man.

As for yourself I am happy that you should have no other knowledge of your sinfulness or of God's goodness but such as you may have wrapped up in the word *sin* or *God* or whatever other word you may choose. In saying this I assume that grace – confirmed by counsel – moves you to it.

But take these words as complete in themselves without speculating on their meaning. In this way your devotion will be kindled, and I believe it should ever be thus in this work.

See Sin as a Lump

Be filled with the spiritual meaning of this word 'sin' without regard to any kind of sin whether venial or mortal: pride, anger, envy, covetousness, sloth, gluttony or lust.

For what does it matter for contemplatives what kind of sin, or how great a sin it is? During the time of this work they will consider all sins equally serious, since the least sin separates from God and hinders their peace.

And feel sin as though it were a lump – of what you never know – but it is none other than yourself. And in the spirit cry out this one cry: SIN, SIN, SIN! OUT, OUT, OUT! This cry of the heart is better learnt from God by experience than from man's teaching.

It is best when it is purely spiritual without any particular thought or pronunciation of words; unless it be but seldom, when – body and soul being filled with the anguish and burden of sin – for very fullness of spirit it erupts into speech.

Our Longing for God Alone

Treat this little word 'God' in the same way. Be filled with the spiritual meaning of the word without consideration of any of God's works, whether material or spiritual, however good they may be, or of any virtue which grace may work in the soul.

Do not think specifically on humility or love, patience or fasting, hope or faith, temperance or love of voluntary poverty. What does this matter to contemplatives who experience all virtue in God?

Such people know that if they have God they have all good, and therefore they long for nothing in particular, but only good God.

You must do likewise so far as grace enables you. Mean God wholly, and wholly mean God, so that nothing works in your mind or will but only God.

A Work without Measure

If you ask what discretion you may have in this work, my answer is none at all! You are to exercise discretion in all your other occupations such as eating or drinking, sleeping or protecting your body from extremes of heat or cold, reading or long praying, or conversation with your fellow-Christians. Use your judgement that these employments be neither too great nor too small. But in *this* work there shall be no measure, for I would that you should never cease from it so long as you live.

I am not saying that you can always come to your work with freshness and vigour. Sometimes sickness or other disorders, or necessities of nature, will draw you down from its perfection. What I do say is that you should experience it either in reality or in spirit; or, to put it otherwise, in actual work or in will. And so, for the love of God, be careful about sickness, so that as far as possible you are not responsible. For I tell you truly, this work demands a calm and peaceful composure, and wholeness and cleanness of body and mind. Take proper care and keep yourself as fit as possible. But if in spite of all, sickness afflicts you, be patient and wait humbly on God's mercy. Nothing more is needed. For I tell you truly that patience in sickness and other trials is often more pleasing to God than any pleasurable devotion you may experience in health.

Avoid Scruples

Perhaps you will ask me how you are to regulate yourself wisely in food and sleep and other such matters. My answer is short: Accept what is offered!

Exercise yourself always without discretion in the work I have set before you, and you will know well enough how to manage properly in other things. I cannot believe that a soul constantly practised in this interior work will err in any of these everyday matters. And if it does, I am bound to think it will always get things wrong.

If I am seriously engaged in this spiritual work within, matters such as eating and drinking, sleeping and speaking will be regarded with an air of indifference. I would prefer to handle them in this way – and so learn discretion – than by a fussy concern which, as it were, kept score of my successes and failures. Believe me, I could never work like that.

So lift up your heart with a blind stirring of love. Use now the word 'sin' and now 'God'. God you would have, and sin you would be without. God you lack, and sin you will. May the good God help you! How greatly you need him!

The Perfection of this Work

Take care that nothing is active in your mind or will but only God. Endeavour to renounce all knowledge and feeling of anything less than God, and tread it well down under the cloud of forgetting.

You must understand that in this work you must not only forget all creatures other than yourself – and all that they and you have done – but you must also forget yourself and what you have done for God. For the perfect lover not only loves the object of his love more than himself, but there is a sense in which he hates himself for the sake of that which he loves.

This is what you must do. You are to hate and grow weary of everything working in your mind and your will, unless it is God alone. Everything else, whatever it is, cannot but be between you and your God.

If you will put what I am saying to the test, you will discover that when you have forgotten all other creatures and all their works – yes, and your own works as well – there will remain within you, between you and your God, a bare knowledge and awareness of your own being. Even this, too, must be overcome before you can truly experience the perfection of this work.

A Word of Warning

Be careful in this exercise that you do not work your-self up emotionally and overtax your strength. Work gladly and eagerly rather than with brute force. The more gladly and lovingly you work, the more humble and spiritual will the work be; whereas the more violently you apply yourself, the more physical and gross will it become. The coarse and vulgar heart which seeks to reach the pinnacle shall be driven off as by stones. And stones are hard and solid things and hurt and bruise painfully.

So be wary of this vulgarity, and learn to love eagerly, behaving gently and modestly in body as in soul. Wait patiently and humbly on our Lord's will, and do not snatch greedily as though you were a famished hound.

And if I may put it somewhat playfully, I advise you to do what is in you to restrain the violent and boisterous stirring of your spirit, pretending that you would hide from him how greatly you want to see him and touch him and hold him.

Perhaps you will think this is childishly and lightly spoken, but I believe that anyone who has the grace to do and feel as I say will find himself caught up in a happy game with him – God kissing and embracing him as a father his child – and would gladly have it so.

The Physical Subject to the Spiritual

❦

I do not say this because I want you at any time to hold back if you feel stirred to vocal prayer. Nor are you to restrain yourself if you have the urge to burst out in an abundance of devotion, speaking to God as to a man and using suitable words as you feel moved: 'Good Jesus! Fair Jesus! Sweet Jesus!' and the like.

God forbid that you should take it thus! Truly I did not mean it so, and God forbid that I should separate body and spirit which he has joined.

Physical things depend on spiritual things and not the opposite.

The subjection of the body to the spirit may be observed by those engaged in the work of this book. For when a man gives himself truly to this work it will quickly happen, although the contemplative himself will not be aware of it, that the body, which for greater ease was tending to stoop, will become upright by virtue of the work of the spirit. Thus the body will correspond physically to the spiritual work in which it is engaged. And quite properly so!

False Contemplatives

Those who are deceived betray themselves by many strange gestures. Anyone watching them as they sit at their work might see them – if their eyes were open – staring as though they were mad, and glowering as if they saw the devil. Well, it's good they should be on their guard; for truly he is not far off!

The eyes of some are set as though they were giddy sheep banged on the head and about to die. Some hang their heads on one side as if a worm were in their ears.

Some squeak when they should speak, as if there were no spirit in their bodies. This is the mark of the hypocrite.

Others wail and splutter in their eagerness and haste to speak their minds. This is the sign of the heretic, and of those who out of presumption and curiosity will always uphold error.

Many disordered and unseemly gestures follow for all to see. Nevertheless there are some astute enough to curb themselves when in the presence of others. But if these men were seen in a place where they might think themselves unobserved, then I believe they would be revealed.

More Strange Antics

Some are so afflicted with odd bodily gestures that when they have to listen to something they hang their heads quaintly on one side, and throw up their chins, gaping as though they would hear with their mouths and not their ears.

Some point when they speak, tapping their fingers or chest; or it may be they poke the chests of those with whom they are speaking.

Some can neither sit still, stand still, nor lie still, unless they are waggling their feet or fidgeting with their hands.

Some speak, making great sweeps with their arms, as if they were to swim across a great stretch of water.

Some are ever smiling or laughing at every word they speak, as though they were wanton women or silly clowns.

Far better is an inner happiness revealing itself in a peaceful countenance and quiet and modest bodily composure.

A Test of Validity

I do not say that all these unseemly gestures are great sins in themselves nor that those who display them are great sinners. I say only that if these ungainly and immoderate gestures become so much a part of man's nature that he cannot shed them at will, then they are tokens of pride and arrogance, and of showing off and an inordinate craving for knowledge.

In particular they are signs of an unstable heart and restless mind and especially of a failure to take to themselves the work of this book. It is only because of this that I have set out so many illustrations of how men may be deceived. Thus, by observing them, those who pursue this work may test the validity of their own practice.

Body and Soul Permeated by this Work

Every man or woman who practises this work will find that it so suffuses body and soul, as to make them gracious and attractive to everyone who sees them.

Indeed, if the least attractive man or woman were drawn by grace to work in this way, their appearance would be quickly changed to one of such graciousness, that all good people who saw them would be glad and happy to have them in their company, and would know that in God's grace they were cheered and strengthened by their presence.

Therefore get this gift – all who by grace may do so. Whoever truly has it will know how to rule himself and all that is his.

He will be wise and perceptive in discerning the character of others. It enables him to be at ease with all who would speak to him – 'saints' and 'sinners' alike – without being drawn into sin himself; and all this to the astonishment of those who see him, and at the same time drawing them through grace to the work in which he is being formed.

The True and the False

The appearance and speech of those who practise this work will be marked by a spiritual wisdom which is both fervent and fruitful. Their words will be spoken in simple sincerity without duplicity, a far cry from the flattering and fawning of hypocrites. These latter devote all their energies, both inward and outward, in discovering how – to prevent themselves looking foolish – they may bolster up their speech, using many 'pious' words and devotional gestures, wanting to appear holy in the sight of men rather than to be so in the sight of God and his angels.

Such people will feel more disgrace and be more upset if caught out in a hurried and unrecollected gesture or in inelegant speech, than for a thousand vanities and sinful impulses wilfully encouraged and carelessly indulged in the sight of God and the saints and the angels in heaven.

Ah, Lord God! Surely pride is harboured within, wherever such mock humility is so plentifully displayed.

When Using Words

When you are alone in prayer, let go all thoughts whether good or bad and attend only to the present moment.

Do not pray aloud unless you have a strong urge to do so. But in case you do use words, count it of no importance whether they are many or few; nor should you allow your mind to deliberate on their meaning.

This rule applies whether you are engaged in petition, praise, hymn or psalm, or indeed any other form of prayer, whether of a particular or general nature; and further it will be so, whether the words are pronounced with your lips or simply formulated in your mind.

Let Him Be as He Is

❦

Let nothing remain in your mind but a naked desire reaching out to God.

Think only that God is as he is. Do not entertain any special thought of God's nature, whether present in himself or in his activity in creation.

Do not search for God by the discursive exercising of your mind; let him be, I say, as he is.

This naked intent, which is to be rooted and grounded freely in faith, will mean for your mind and emotions a bare conception and a blind awareness of your own being.

It will be as if you were to say to him: That which I am, Lord, I offer to you. I do not consider any attribute of your nature, but only that you are as you are, that and no more.

God Is God and You Are You

You must think of God in this work as you think of yourself, and of yourself as you think of God: that God is as he is, and that you are as you are.

Such simplification of thought means that your mind will not be scattered or separated from God, but joined to him who is all.

There will, however, always be this difference between you and him, that he is your being, and not you his.

Look up, then, joyously and say to your Lord either in word or desire: 'That which I am, Lord, I give to you, for you are as you are.' And reflect simply, sincerely, and ardently that you are as you are – that and no more – without any trace of speculative inquiry.

Consider Only that You Are

Surely a man would need to be dull witted beyond all measure if he could not understand and experience that he is – note that I do not say that he is to understand what he is, but simply that he is.

So I urge you to let go all complexity of thought and to think in the simplest manner not what you are, but that you are.

This which I now bid you do you have indeed done for some while with the help of grace, and I will allow that it may be profitable to you at this time to know in part what you are: a man by nature and a shameful wretch by sin – in what manner you well know.

It may be that you sometimes dwell too much on the defilement which surrounds and clings to a fallen creature. Away with all this! I beg you, let it all go! Stop such muck-raking lest the stench overcomes you!

But to think instead just this – *that you are* – this you may do artlessly and simply without scholarship or natural learning.

A Poultice to Your Sick Self

Take good, gracious God as he is, and lay him as a poultice on your sick self as you are. Or, if I may put it otherwise, begin with your disordered self and, just as you are, reach out in desire to touch good, gracious God as he is.

Do we not know from the gospels that simply to touch God is endless health? 'If I but touch the hem of his garment I shall be healed': so said the woman who came to him. Much more then shall you be healed of the sickness of your soul by this lovely heavenly touching of God himself.

Step out then resolutely and apply this sovereign remedy. Just as you are, lift up your sick self to God as he is – our God is good and gracious.

Do this without introspection concerning yourself, without speculation concerning God. Forget all about concepts like clean or unclean, spiritual or material, divine or human. All that now matters is that, stripped of all conceptual thought, you contemplate God in the eager longing of love. So shall you be graciously united in spirit to the lovely being of God himself – God as he is – that and no more.

Everything Contained in the Word 'Is'

In this work you may no more turn your attention to the attributes of God's being than to those of your own.

For if you look at God in the perspective of eternity there is no name you can give him – nor is there any experience or understanding – which is more fitting (for this work) than that which is contained in the blind and lovely beholding of the word *is*.

For example, if you call God good or fair, or sweet, merciful or righteous, wise or omniscient, mighty or almighty, intelligent or wise, might or strength, love or charity, or whatever else it might be, it is all contained in this one short word *is*.

And though you add a hundred thousand words such as good, fair and all the rest, you never get further than this one word. You do not add to it if you say them all. You do not take away from it if you say none.

Leaving all considerations behind, offer yourself to God, the whole of you as you are, to all of him as he is.

Our Varying Capacities for this Work

There are some who regard this task as so formidable and daunting that they think that it cannot be achieved without much hard and persevering preliminary work. Even then, they would say, they experience it but rarely and then only in moments of ecstasy.

I would answer such men as humbly as I can by saying that it all rests entirely on the decree and good pleasure of God, who gives every man the grace of contemplation and spiritual working according to his capacity to receive it.

There are some who will not achieve it without long and arduous spiritual labour. It will be but seldom, and then only by virtue of God's special calling, that they will experience the perfection of this work.

On the other hand there are others so attuned in grace and spirit, and so at home with God in this grace of contemplation, that they may have it when they please in the ordinary occupations of life as in sitting, walking, standing or kneeling. And, yet, during this time they have full control of their faculties and may exercise them if they wish; not, it is true, without some difficulty, but without great difficulty.

This Way Is Not for All

❦

If you think that you are physically or spiritually temperamentally unsuited to this work, you may leave it for some other way. Under good direction there will be no danger and you are not to feel guilty about it. In that case I ask you to excuse me. As far as my limited knowledge allows, I have only wanted to help you.

However, read over what I have written two or three times; the more often the better, and the more you will understand. It may well be that some sentence which presented difficulties at the first or second reading will later become clear.

If a man is truly disposed to this work I think it must be that in the reading or speaking of it, or in hearing it read or spoken, he will feel a positive drawing to what it is doing for him. If then you think it is doing you good, thank God with all your heart and in your love for God pray for me.

If there is anything I have written which you would like clarified or developed, let me know together with your own views. I will endeavour to explain it as best I can.

The Test of Vocation

Those who come to know this book must not think that God is calling them to its work simply because they feel warmly attracted to it at the time of their reading. Their feelings may arise from a natural curiosity of mind rather than the calling of grace.

Those who wish to test their calling should first ask whether everything has been done for the cleansing of conscience as the Church requires, and in the following of the counsel given.

Then, if they wish to know more surely, let them ask if they have been inwardly stirred to this work more constantly than to any other spiritual exercise.

If they then think that everything they do, whether physical or spiritual, lacks the approval of their conscience unless this secret little love, pressing upon the cloud of unknowing, is in a spiritual manner the mainstay of all their work, then it is a sign that they are called of God; otherwise it is not so.

The Withdrawal of Feelings

I do not say, however, that those who are called to this work will continually experience the stirring of God's love, for that will not be so.

The beginner in contemplation will often experience the withdrawal of the support of his feelings, and there are various reasons for this.

One reason why agreeable feelings are withdrawn in prayer is lest the beginner should presume upon them and imagine it to be largely within his control to have them as and when he likes.

Pride, which is at the root of such thoughts, is the reason for God's withdrawal of these pleasurable feelings. I am speaking of latent and not actual pride, the pride that would have been occasioned if the feelings had been allowed to remain.

Foolish young people often imagine that this makes God their enemy; whereas in fact he is most fully their friend.

A True and Certain Sign

Carelessness is sometimes the cause of the with-drawal of the feelings of those who practise this work. Such people suffer bitterly and grievously when this is so.

Our Lord will sometimes deliberately keep one waiting in this matter of sensible pleasure. This is because by delaying it he will cause it to grow, and be more highly valued when it is eventually restored after prolonged absence.

It is one of the clearest and most easily discernible signs by which one may know whether one is called to this work or not: if one finds after long delay that when the feelings of grace are suddenly given back – and in no sense earned – that one's fervour has grown, and one's love and longing for the work are greater than ever before.

One often has more delight in finding refreshment anew than one ever had grief in its loss.

If these things are so, it is a true and unquestion-able sign that one is called by God to pursue this work, whatever one is or has been.

Holly Desires Grow by Delays

God in his mercy looks on you not for what you are, nor for what you have been, but for what you wish to be.

St Gregory tells us that all holy desires grow by delays, and that if instead they die away, then in the first place they were never holy. For if a man feels ever less and less delight in new discoveries and in the unexpected resurgence of former desires, although he may have had a *natural* desire for what is good, *holy* it never was.

St Augustine says that the life of a Christian is nothing else but holy desire.

Farewell, spiritual friend, with God's blessing and mine! I pray Almighty God that true peace, wise counsel and spiritual comfort in God with abundance of grace, may be with you always and with all God's lovers upon earth. Amen.

The Call to Contemplation

꩜

There comes a time in the lives of many people when the way of discursive meditation is no longer satisfying. Even more than that it becomes very difficult, if not practically impossible, for them to use it in their prayer time. If this development is accompanied by a deep longing for God, if we find ourselves just wanting him and him alone, then we may take this as an indication that the Holy Spirit is leading us to contemplative prayer, and we must be content to leave meditation behind and yield to the impress of the Spirit.

'Like as the hart desireth the water brooks, so longeth my soul after thee, O God.' 'When I awake after thy likeness, I shall be satisfied.' Settled or returning aspirations such as these may be taken as sure signs of the contemplative call.

At the same time everyday things are likely to become less satisfying than before. There may perhaps be some withdrawal, though in the end we shall be likely to come back to all the good things of God's creation, but in a different way – they will now be caught up in the love of God and become the overflow of prayer into daily life.

I am describing what is a well-trodden path in the pilgrimage of the spirit. St John of the Cross is the authority usually referred to, and he gives the signs three times in his writings.

Many will recognize this as a stage in their own lives, perhaps many years ago. But just as, when one is motoring into unexpected country and has no map, one is worried lest one has lost the way, so some people – when the old ways of prayer are no longer possible – become worried and discouraged. And because the silent ways in which they are now drawn involve such simplifications of memory and mind and will, they may begin to ask whether they are now really praying at all. Very possibly they now try to turn back to the old way, and finding it fruitless they are tempted to give up altogether.

This is where knowledge of the well-worn paths of the Spirit may reinforce our faith and enable us to persevere. What is happening is neatly summarized in this short definition by Father Stanton, which distinguishes meditation from contemplation: 'Meditation is a detachment from the things of the world in order to attend to the things of God. Contemplation is a detachment from the things of God in order to attend to God himself.'

(The Compiler)

A Reality Known by Faith Alone

In meditation, a great effort is made to build up, assemble ideas, take resolutions. This effort is very good, but it is a human effort. In prayer a man presents himself before God and remains there in all his weakness, but also with love and an open heart, and it is the Holy Spirit who directs the conversation. It is true that this conversation takes place in the depths of the soul beyond the realm of consciousness, and faith alone tells us that this dialogue is taking place. At the end of the thirty or sixty minutes passed thus in the silence of love, we shall perhaps be under the impression that we have been battling against distractions and even yielding most of the time. But our faith affirms that the Holy Spirit is at work here, and that his action in us is far more important than all the words we might have uttered . . .

> We pray, not in order to gather strength, but to offer our strength to God. We pray, not in order to receive, but to give to God, to give without realizing we are giving, to give without joy, if need be, and in the darkness to deliver up our being and our life.

(Gérard Huyghe)

Resting in God's Presence

🎺

Prayer, especially undistracted prayer does not grow easier as I grow older. The mere mental effort is sometimes exceedingly hard; but the will to pray trained by long habit is stronger, and the conviction that prayer is my primary service has been re-enforced. I know now, beyond a doubt that my best means of glorifying God, usually my sole means, is in prayer, whether mental or vocal, or the mere acceptance of suffering. The silent, almost imperceptible union with God's will and my ceding all to him give the hours meaning. Habitually arid, I offer my distractions, sure that God knows not only that they are not of my choosing but also that they render me more conscious of my littleness. With God we are always children no matter how old we are. And sometimes in dry prayer I find myself as powerless as a baby, as utterly unable to think as I was in infancy, not even competent to offer a petition save the almost automatic 'God have mercy'. And with the experience of years I know there is nothing to do but to rest in God's presence as a baby does in its mother's arms. And, after all, rest has a place in the spiritual life.

(Mary Hope)

The Healing of the Memories

❦

Compiler's note. The following passage links closely with the reading on page 40 of this book. Readers who are interested in this important aspect of prayer will find it discussed in relation to *The Cloud of Unknowing* in chapters 11 and 12 of my book *With Pity Not with Blame*, (DLT 1982).

As the contemplative life develops, it simplifies. Words become fewer; silence predominates; inner words rise up from the deeper areas of the psyche and from the centre of the soul. And at this time other things also surface from the unconscious, things that need to be healed – suppressed fears, anguish, all kinds of hurts. Now one continues to sit in the presence of God in a situation that is paradoxically filled with joy and filled with anguish. Here there is a strange mixture of peace and pain.

And this is the beginning of the dark night. Now I must not push these hurts into the unconscious; I must not bury them; I must not flee from the ghosts and the dragons and the wild beasts that leer and smirk and grimace. It does not help to run away either to watch television or to play golf or to throw myself into frenetic work. However laudable these activities in themselves, now is not the time for them. Now is the time to sit quietly with God even when the whole inner life becomes desperately painful, even when all hell seems to break loose inside me. I must let it all surface. I must face the devil. But (and this is important) while I *watch* all this material as it comes up, I must not *analyse* it or *get involved* with it. I must not be seduced by the wild figures from the unconscious; I must not let them engage me in treacherous dialogue. No, no. I must remain with God in the cloud of unknowing, simply watching them and watching myself with compassion.

Painful, you will say. Yes, very painful . . . But the suffering and pain need not disturb me. It has to be so. There seems to be a direct relationship between healing and suffering. In order to be healed one must suffer . . . And through this painful process the memory is being healed. The hurts and pains that have been lurking in the psyche from early child-hood, from the moment of birth, from the time in the womb, from the moment of conception – all of these are floating to the surface and are being healed by the love of the indwelling Spirit in whose presence one quietly sits.

(William Johnston, SJ)

Some Thoughts on Faith and Prayer

By pure faith I mean that state in which one serves God without any pledge or assurance of being pleasing to him. This state is extremely painful to self-love, and so it must be for it is meant to undermine it imperceptibly and in the end to destroy it so far as is possible in this life.

(J. N. Grou)

There is no progress in prayer without progress in faith, a purification of faith. And this entails a removal of all the props which depend on human endeavour, human reasoning, signs and the rest. It is the naked faith which is a terrifying experience and yet is the meeting point ultimately between God and ourselves in the depth of our being. This experience of the purification of faith is not normally one which comes early in religious life. It comes late.

We may wonder sometimes what is the result of our fidelity to prayer. From day to day there is little result that we can see or assess. Only when one looks back over the years does one come to realize that our convictions concerning the things of God are, despite all, clearer than they were. And I think finally that the most important result of our fidelity to prayer is that, despite everything, we want to go on praying.

(Basil Hume)

An Idiotic State

The late Dom John Chapman, Abbot of Downside, writes: 'This time of prayer is passed in the act of wanting God. It is an idiotic state and feels like the completest waste of time until it gradually becomes more vivid. The strangest phenomenon is when we begin to wonder whether we mean anything at all, and whether we are addressing anyone, or merely repeating mechanically a formula we do not mean. The word, God, seems to mean nothing. If we feel this curious and paradoxical condition we are starting on the right road, and we must beware of trying to think what God is and what he has done for us, etc., because this takes us out of prayer and spoils God's work . . .' It is deliberate thinking which stops intuitive contemplation. Thoughts may well go on automatically as a background to contemplation without our willing it. All we can do is to ignore them as far as possible, perhaps with the help of some verbal formula as suggested earlier. The abbot insisted that the person who in prayer renounced all deliberate thinking must think about the things of God when not praying. He needs to consecrate not only his intuition but his reason, imagination and common sense. These other faculties may be enlisted through reading, writing or speaking which brings them into play as well as by practical action in the service of other people.

(Christopher Bryant)

Index and Acknowledgement of Sources

❦

The basic book on *The Cloud* in Middle English is edited by Phyllis Hodgson and published by the Oxford University Press for the Early English Text Society. Its full title is *The Cloud of Unknowing and the Book of Privy Counselling*. Those who like to read *The Cloud* in the idiom and syntax of the Middle English, but with the spelling modernized, may be referred to the work entitled *The Cloud of Unknowing together with the Epistle of Privy Counsel*, edited by Abbot Justin McCann, OSB (Burns and Oates). I gratefully acknowledge the help of both books in my rendering of the text into modern English.

Those who desire the full text in modern English may care to refer to *The Cloud of Unknowing and Other Works* edited by Clifton Wolters in the Penguin Classics series; or to *The Cloud of Unknowing* edited by James Walsh, SJ and published by the SPCK in the series, The Classics of Western Spirituality; or to *The Cloud of Unknowing* edited by Ira Progoff and published by Rider and Company. I am gratefully indebted to these books in addition to those earlier mentioned. It should be noted that only the first of these latter three contains *The Book of Privy Counsel* as well as *The Cloud*. The third book is especially valuable for the psychological insights which its introduction sheds upon *The Cloud.*

The index overleaf shows the chapters from which the readings have been taken. The page reference in this book is shown in bold and is followed by the chapter numbers in *The Cloud of Unknowing* (CU) or *The Book of Privy Counsel* (PC).

R.L.

69 Robert Llewelyn, *Prayer and Contemplation*. SLG Press, Fairacres, Oxford, 1975.

71 Gérard Huyghe, *Tension and Change*, tr. Sister Marie Florette, SCH. Geoffrey Chapman, a division of Cassells Ltd, 1967.

72 Mary Hope, *Towards Evening*. Sheed and Ward. © Mary Hope 1974.

73 William Johnston, SJ, *The Mirror Mind*. Collins. © William Johnston 1981.

75 Basil Hume, *Searching for God*. © Hodder and Stoughton, 1977.

76 Christopher Bryant, *The River Within*. Darton, Longman and Todd, 1978.

Thanks are due to the above mentioned for permission to reproduce material from copyright sources.